MY CRAZY INVENTIONS SKETCHBOOK

ANDREW RAE & LISA REGAN

LAURENCE KING PUBLISHING

PUBLISHED IN 2015
LAURENCE KING PUBLISHING
AN IMPRINT OF
HACHETTE CHILDREN'S GROUP
PART OF HODDER AND STOUGHTON
CARMELITE HOUSE
50 VICTORIA EMBANKMENT
LONDON EC4Y 0DZ

© 2015 LAURENCE KING PUBLISHING LTD
THIS BOOK WAS DESIGNED AND PRODUCED BY
LAURENCE KING PUBLISHING LTD, LONDON.

ILLUSTRATIONS © 2015 ANDREW RAE

TEXT © 2015 LISA REGAN

A CATALOG RECORD FOR THIS BOOK IS
AVAILABLE FROM THE BRITISH LIBRARY.

ISBN: 978-1-78067-611-1

DESIGN: ALEXANDRE COCO

PRINTED IN CHINA

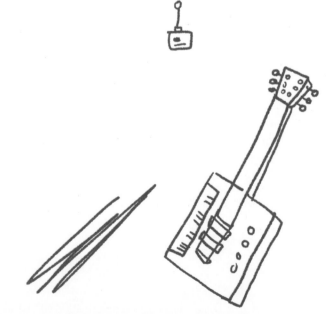

MY CRAZY INVENTIONS SKETCHBOOK

ANDREW RAE & LISA REGAN

GETTING STARTED

EVEN THE MOST BONKERS IDEAS SOMETIMES MAKE IT INTO THE REAL WORLD. WHETHER THESE INVENTIONS ARE USEFUL OR NOT IS A DIFFERENT MATTER – BUT IT'S DARING TO DREAM THAT SETS HUMANS APART FROM OTHER CREATURES. GREAT INVENTORS HAVE TO BE PREPARED TO TRY – AND FAIL – AND STILL KEEP TRYING. HERE ARE SOME TOP TIPS...

TOP TIP NO.1

LEARN TO LET GO
NO MATTER HOW GREAT YOU THINK YOUR IDEA IS, IF NO ONE ELSE AGREES – EVER – THEN IT'S NOT GOING TO CHANGE THE WORLD OR MAKE YOU A MILLIONAIRE. SOME PATENTED IDEAS NEVER GET MADE, SUCH AS US PATENT 2882858, 'A DIAPER FOR BIRDS'. TIDY!

TOP TIP NO.2

KEEP A NOTEBOOK
YOUR SKETCHES, PLANS, THOUGHTS, NOTES, AND WEBLINKS ARE ALL IMPORTANT. ONE OF THE WORLD'S GREATEST INVENTORS, LEONARDO DA VINCI (1452–1519), CARRIED A NOTEBOOK EVERYWHERE HE WENT, AND LEFT A WHOPPING 13,000 PAGES OF SCRIBBLES WHEN HE DIED!

fig 3.

a

b

c

d

e

f

g

TOP
TIP
NO.3

CHECK IT OUT

MAKE SURE YOU'RE NOT INVENTING SOMETHING THAT ALREADY EXISTS.
GOT A GREAT PLAN TO PUT BUTTER IN A GLUE STICK? ALREADY BEEN
DONE... CHECK OUT THE END OF THE BOOK WHERE WE EXPLAIN ALL
ABOUT PATENTS.

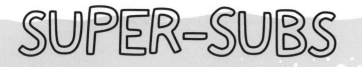

SUPER-SUBS

WHAT WOULD YOUR SUB LOOK LIKE IF YOU INVENTED ONE?

SUBMARINES ARE COOL, BUT ONE THAT LOOKS LIKE A SHARK IS EVEN COOLER, RIGHT?

THE 'SEABREACHER X' CAN CARRY TWO PEOPLE, AND LEAP RIGHT OUT OF THE WATER TO DO TWISTS AND ROLLS!

AND IF YOU PREFER PLANES TO SHARKS, HERE YOU GO: THERE'S A SUBMARINE THAT FLIES THROUGH THE WATER LIKE A PLANE, COMPLETE WITH WINGS AND STEERING SYSTEM. THE 'SAS SUPER AVIATOR' IS USED FOR OCEAN RESEARCH AND CAN DIVE TO 1,000 FEET.

DOGGY DOOS

RAINING CATS AND DOGS?

NOT A PROBLEM: BUY A DOG UMBRELLA!

INVENTIONS AREN'T JUST FOR HUMANS, YOU KNOW...

WHAT WOULD YOU CALL AN INVENTION TO PROTECT YOUR POOCH'S EYES?

'DOGGLES', OF COURSE! THEY KEEP OUT DIRT AND WIND AND OFFER UV PROTECTION.

WANT TO KNOW WHAT YOUR DOG'S BARKING ABOUT?

YOU NEED A 'BOW-LINGUAL' DOG-TO-HUMAN TRANSLATION DEVICE! THE 'BOW-LINGUAL' STRAPS ON TO A COLLAR AND FLASHES UP PHRASES ONTO A HANDSET, DEPENDING ON WHETHER THE DOG'S BARKING IS HAPPY, SAD, OR ON GUARD.

KEEP-FIT FOR DOGS! DOES YOUR DOG RUN AND RUN? HARNESS THAT DOG POWER WITH A DOG-POWERED SCOOTER! SOMEBODY ACTUALLY INVENTED THIS!

THE INVENTORS OF THESE TWO PRODUCTS WANTED A DOG IN THEIR LIFE, WITHOUT THE MESS. WE PRESENT TO YOU... THE 'NEATER FEEDER' AND THE 'POOPSTA'! CAN YOU GUESS WHAT THEY'RE DESIGNED TO DO?

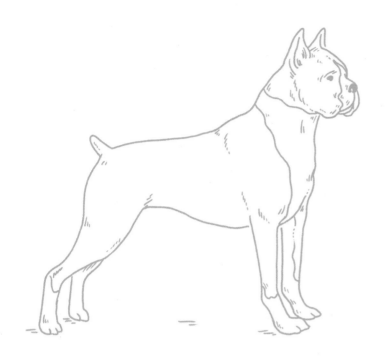

KEEP THESE DOGS HAPPY WITH
SOME CANINE CONTRAPTIONS.

FIT FOR ANYTHING

FANCY A SWIM BUT DON'T WANT TO GET WET?

TRAIN ON DRY LAND WITH A SWIM MACHINE THAT ALLOWS YOU TO PRACTICE ANYWHERE, BY PEDALING WITH YOUR ARMS AND USING A KIND OF STAIR CLIMBER FOR YOUR LEG STROKES. THIS ONE HZAS BEEN PATENTED BUT IS NOT YET AVAILABLE IN A STORE NEAR YOU...

HATS OFF TO YOU!

USE YOUR HEAD, LIKE THE INVENTORS OF THESE DEVICES DID.

THIS INVENTOR WAS A HAY FEVER SUFFERER WHO JUST NEVER HAD A TISSUE HANDY WHEN THE SNIFFLES STRUCK...

MP3 PLAYERS ARE GREAT FOR MUSIC ON THE MOVE, BUT THEY DON'T KEEP YOUR HEAD WARM... PROBLEM SOLVED WITH THIS RADIO IN A HAT!

THE BOWLER HAT WAS INVENTED FOR GAMEKEEPERS AS AN ALTERNATIVE TO THE TALL TOP HAT, WHICH WAS EASILY KNOCKED OFF WHEN RIDING THROUGH TREES.

ROBERT W. PATTEN PATENTED THIS PROTECTIVE HAT IN 1880. HE BECAME KNOWN AS 'THE UMBRELLA MAN'.

THE 'BEER HELMET' - A HAT THAT HOLDS DRINKS CANS AND A FLEXIBLE STRAW SO YOU CAN DRINK HANDS-FREE - WAS INVENTED IN 1983 BY BUFFALO BILLS FAN JEREMY GUMBO.

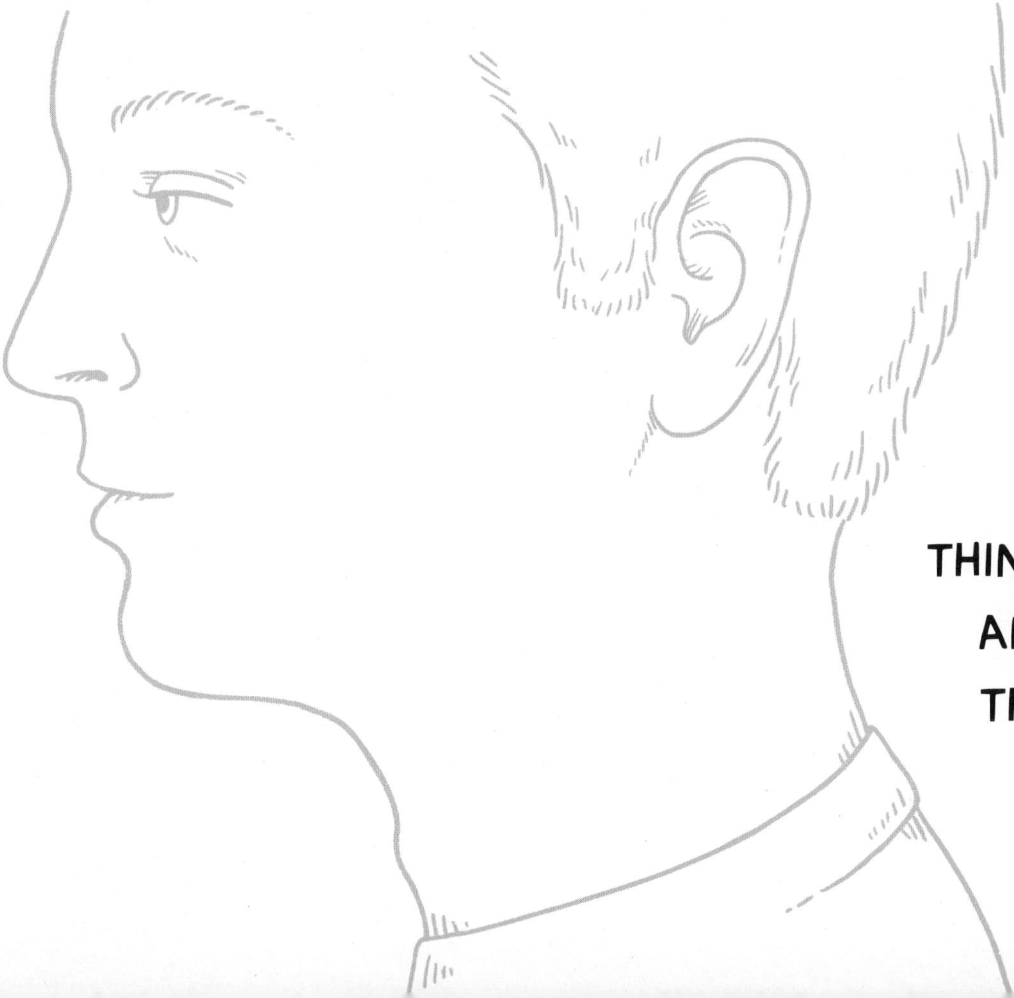

PUT YOUR
THINKING CAP ON
AND CUSTOMIZE
THIS HEADWEAR.

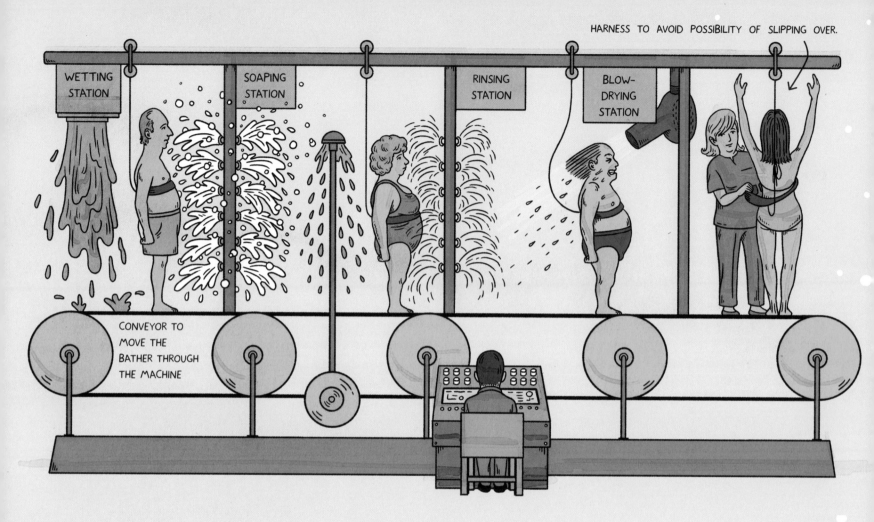

HARNESS TO AVOID POSSIBILITY OF SLIPPING OVER.

WETTING STATION

SOAPING STATION

RINSING STATION

BLOW-DRYING STATION

CONVEYOR TO MOVE THE BATHER THROUGH THE MACHINE

CAR WASH FOR PEOPLE

THE 'HUMAN CAR WASH' (HCW) WAS PATENTED IN 1969 AND ITS SUGGESTED USES INCLUDED 'MASS BATHING AFTER AN ATOMIC BOMB'.

WILLIAM BLACKSTONE FROM INDIANA, USA, DESIGNED A CLOTHES WASHING MACHINE IN 1874 AS A BIRTHDAY PRESENT FOR HIS WIFE. SOOOO MUCH BETTER THAN CHOCOLATES; SHE MUST HAVE BEEN THRILLED.

INVENT A MACHINE
THAT CAN GET YOU CLEAN!

HOLD ON!

THE ART OF INVENTION INCLUDES SOLVING UNIQUE PROBLEMS THAT JUST DON'T OCCUR TO MOST PEOPLE... LIKE THESE TENTS DESIGNED TO HANG ON THE SIDE OF A CLIFF.

DON'T LOOK DOWN!

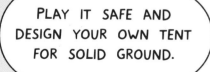

PLAY IT SAFE AND DESIGN YOUR OWN TENT FOR SOLID GROUND.

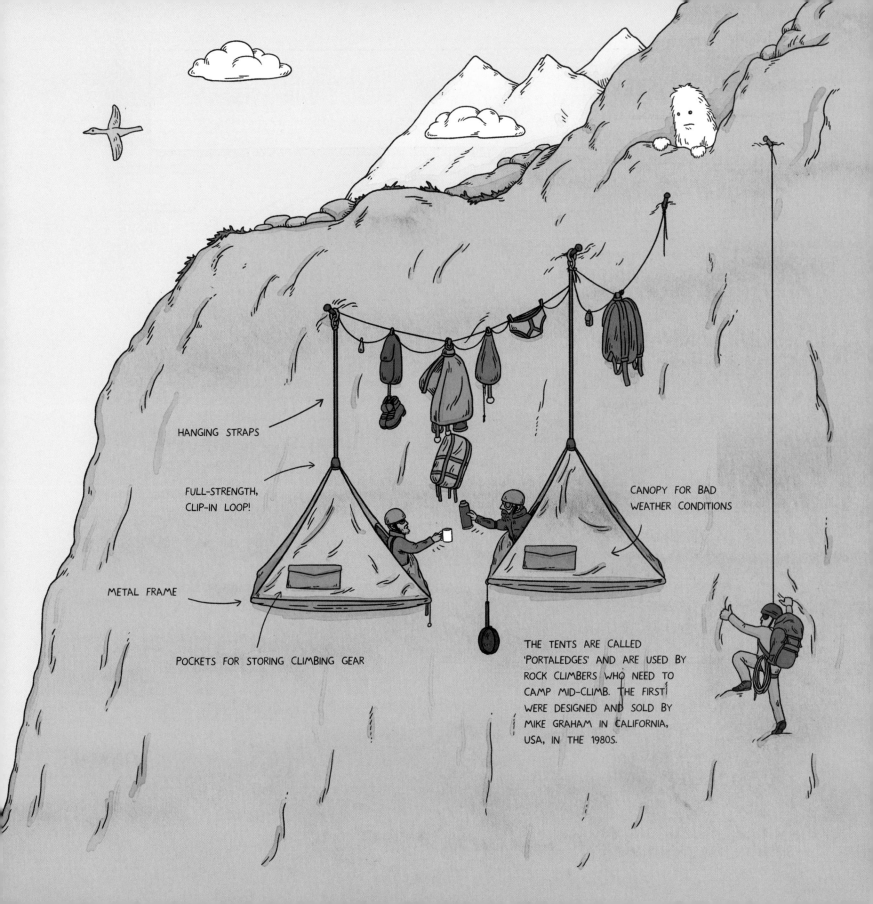

HANGING STRAPS

FULL-STRENGTH,
CLIP-IN LOOP!

CANOPY FOR BAD
WEATHER CONDITIONS

METAL FRAME

POCKETS FOR STORING CLIMBING GEAR

THE TENTS ARE CALLED
'PORTALEDGES' AND ARE USED BY
ROCK CLIMBERS WHO NEED TO
CAMP MID-CLIMB. THE FIRST
WERE DESIGNED AND SOLD BY
MIKE GRAHAM IN CALIFORNIA,
USA, IN THE 1980S.

DID YOU KNOW THAT THE NAME OF THE TIME-TRAVEL
MACHINE IN 'DOCTOR WHO' - THE TARDIS - STANDS FOR
'TIME AND RELATIVE DIMENSION IN SPACE'?

WHAT WOULD YOUR
TIME-TRAVEL MACHINE LOOK LIKE?

SO SIMPLE...

SOME OF THE BEST INVENTIONS ARE INCREDIBLY SIMPLE, LIKE THESE:

THE FIRST SHOES DESIGNED SPECIFICALLY FOR RUNNING WERE PRODUCED IN 1895.

M&M'S WERE INVENTED DURING THE SPANISH CIVIL WAR (1936-39) WHEN FORREST MARS SAW SOLDIERS EATING CHOCOLATE THAT WAS COVERED WITH A HARD COATING TO STOP IT FROM MELTING IN THE SUN.

VELCRO IS ACTUALLY JUST MATERIAL WITH TINY HOOKS AND LOOPS THAT CATCH TOGETHER. THE DESIGN, BY SWISS ENGINEER GEORGE DE MESTRAL IN THE 1940S, WAS INVENTED WHEN HE NOTICED THE WAY HOOKED PLANT SEEDS KEPT GETTING STUCK TO HIS DOG'S COAT!

SQUEEZY KETCHUP

CANS FOR STORING FOOD WERE FIRST INVENTED IN 1810. BUT THE FIRST CAN OPENER WAS ONLY PATENTED AND PRODUCED NEARLY 50 YEARS LATER!

CAN'T GET THE KETCHUP OUT OF THE GLASS BOTTLE? DESIGN A SQUEEZY BOTTLE, ESPECIALLY FOR SAUCE!

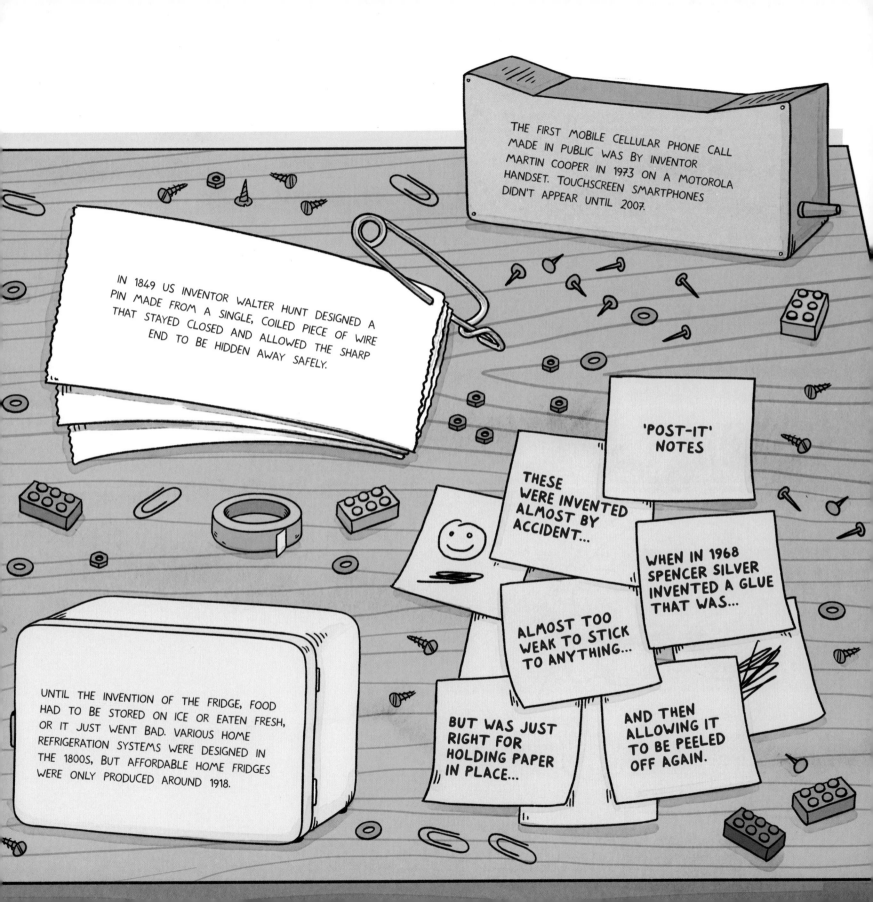

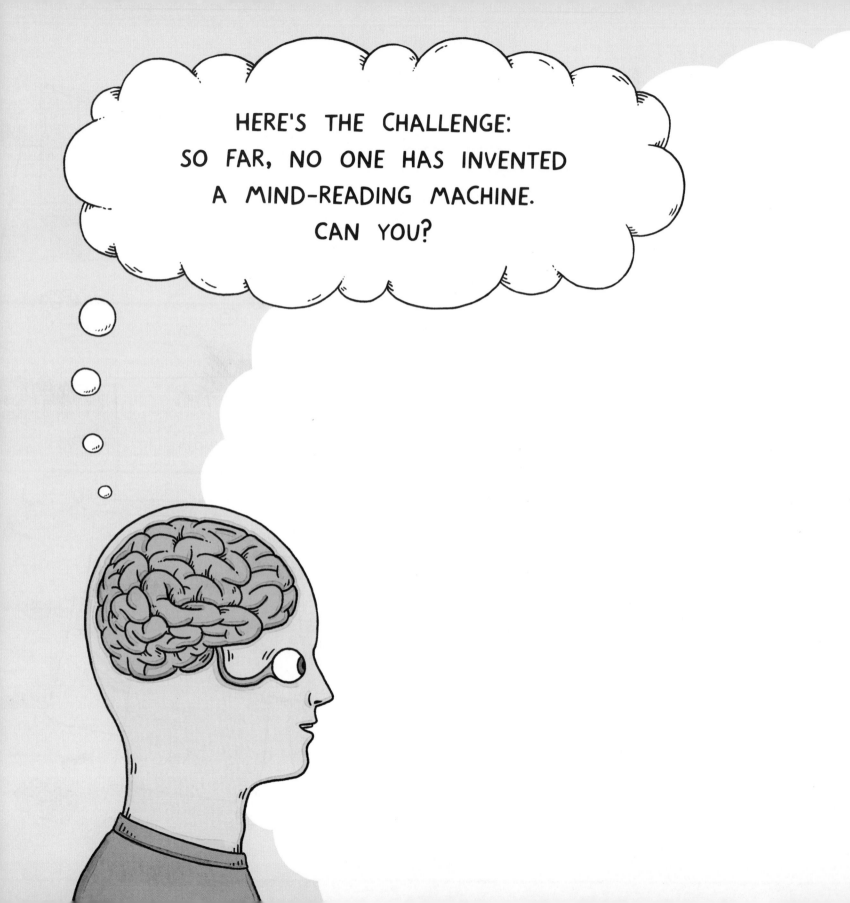

SPACE PLANE

FANCY A QUICK FLIGHT INTO SPACE?
IT'S POSSIBLE!

'SPACESHIPONE' WAS THE FIRST COMMERCIAL VEHICLE
TO CARRY PEOPLE INTO SPACE (COMMERCIAL MEANING
IT WAS DEVELOPED WITH PRIVATE FUNDING INSTEAD
OF GOVERNMENT MONEY). IT FLEW IN 2004, AND
THAT YEAR WON A PRIZE FROM THE 'XPRIZE
FOUNDATION', INTENDED TO ENCOURAGE LOW-COST
SPACE FLIGHT. WE HAVE LIFT-OFF!

SEE-ANYTHING GLASSES

WHATEVER THE WEATHER

IT'S ALWAYS BEST TO BE PREPARED FOR A DOWNPOUR.

HANDLE THE RAIN WITH
AN INVENTOR'S GENIUS, AND
CAPTURE WATER FOR RE-USE.
HERE ARE TWO SUGGESTIONS.

CAN YOU COME UP WITH A
WACKY WEATHER CREATION?

TIRED OF WALKING?

TAKE A SEAT - LITERALLY.
LIKE, TAKE IT WITH YOU.

DESIGNER JOOYOUN PAEK HAS CREATED A DRESS
THAT INFLATES INTO A CHAIR, SO YOU CAN TAKE A
SEAT ANYWHERE. IT CONNECTS TO AIR PUMP SHOES
THAT INFLATE THE SKIRT UNTIL IT BECOMES A
COMFORTABLE PERCHING POST. AND... RELAX.

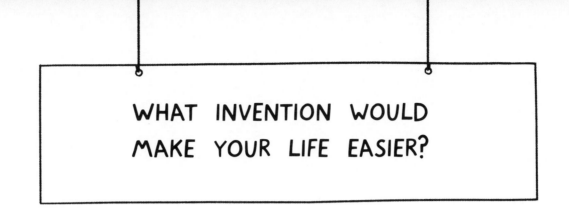

WHAT INVENTION WOULD
MAKE YOUR LIFE EASIER?

UNPLUGGED

CAN'T FIND AN ELECTRICAL OUTLET
TO CHARGE YOUR PHONE? NO PROBLEM...

HOW WOULD YOU
CHARGE THIS PHONE?

SIXTEEN-YEAR-OLD INVENTOR PETER ASH
TURNED HIS SISTER'S HAMSTER WHEEL INTO
A PHONE CHARGER. RUN, HAMMY, RUN!

TRANSFORMERS

FIRST THERE WAS THE CARTOON, AND THEN
THERE WAS... AARGH! A REAL-LIFE ONE!

YES, A MAN IN BRAZIL HAS REALLY,
TRULY BUILT A MACHINE THAT CHANGES
FROM VAN TO ROBOT AND THEN BACK
TO A VAN AGAIN. IT TAKES AROUND TWO
MINUTES TO TRANSFORM.

PLAN YOUR BEFORE-AND-AFTER
LOOK FOR A REAL-LIFE
TRANSFORMER.

IT'S RAINING, IT'S POURING

DON'T BE SILLY - NO ONE INVENTED RAIN.
HOWEVER, PEOPLE HAVE TRIED TO INVENT RAIN MACHINES...

SCIENTISTS IN THE 1960S DID FIND A WAY TO
INTERFERE WITH THE STRUCTURE OF CLOUDS
TO BRING ON SHOWERS. SENDING UP ROCKETS
OR PLANES TO ADD SUBSTANCES TO THE AIR
CAN INCREASE RAINFALL. THE PROCESS - CALLED
'CLOUD SEEDING' - CAN ALSO BE DONE FROM
THE GROUND. NO MORE RAIN DANCING!

WHAT WOULD YOUR WEATHER
MACHINE LOOK LIKE?

AND TODAY'S CHALLENGE IS...

CAN YOU INVENT THE BEST DUNE
BUGGY EVER? HOW ABOUT COMBINING
IT WITH AN ICE-CREAM VAN?
SUN, SAND, AND STRAWBERRY SAUCE!

ROBOTIC FRIENDS

OKAY, SO ROBOTIC ARMS BUILD CARS. BUT WE WANT ONES THAT DANCE AND PLAY PING-PONG!

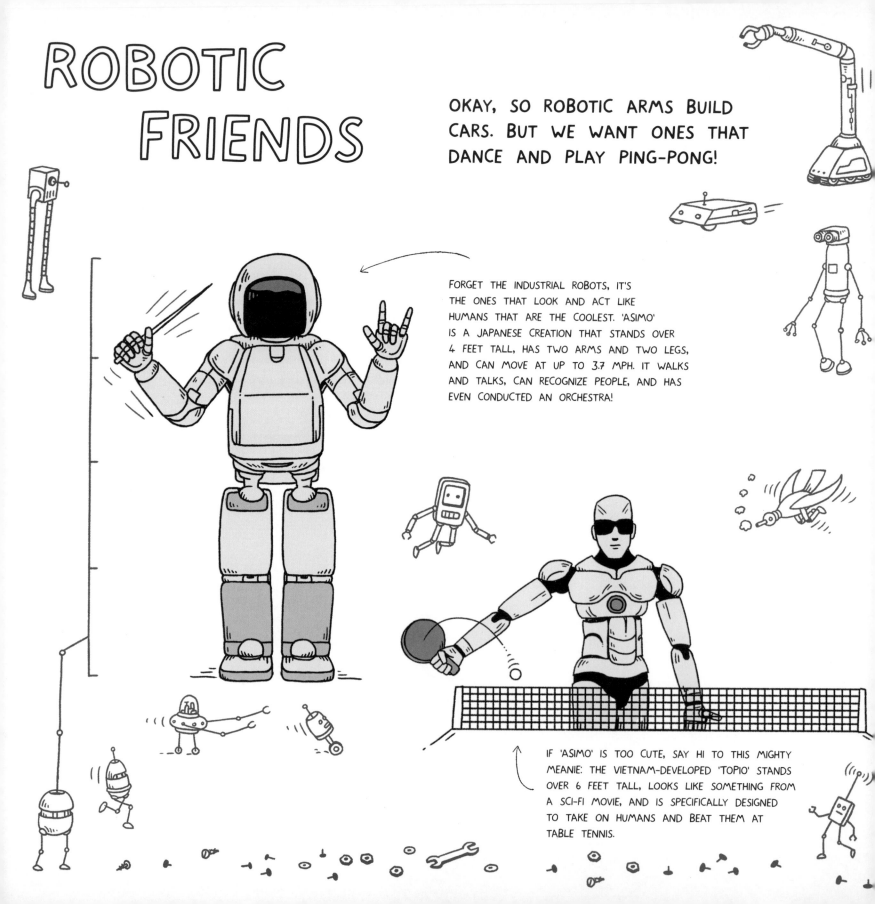

FORGET THE INDUSTRIAL ROBOTS, IT'S THE ONES THAT LOOK AND ACT LIKE HUMANS THAT ARE THE COOLEST. 'ASIMO' IS A JAPANESE CREATION THAT STANDS OVER 4 FEET TALL, HAS TWO ARMS AND TWO LEGS, AND CAN MOVE AT UP TO 3.7 MPH. IT WALKS AND TALKS, CAN RECOGNIZE PEOPLE, AND HAS EVEN CONDUCTED AN ORCHESTRA!

IF 'ASIMO' IS TOO CUTE, SAY HI TO THIS MIGHTY MEANIE: THE VIETNAM-DEVELOPED 'TOPIO' STANDS OVER 6 FEET TALL, LOOKS LIKE SOMETHING FROM A SCI-FI MOVIE, AND IS SPECIFICALLY DESIGNED TO TAKE ON HUMANS AND BEAT THEM AT TABLE TENNIS.

DRAW THE COOLEST ROBOT
YOU CAN COME UP WITH.

INVISIBILITY CLOAK

WOULDN'T YOU JUST LOVE TO BE ABLE TO DISAPPEAR WHEN YOU'RE IN TROUBLE?

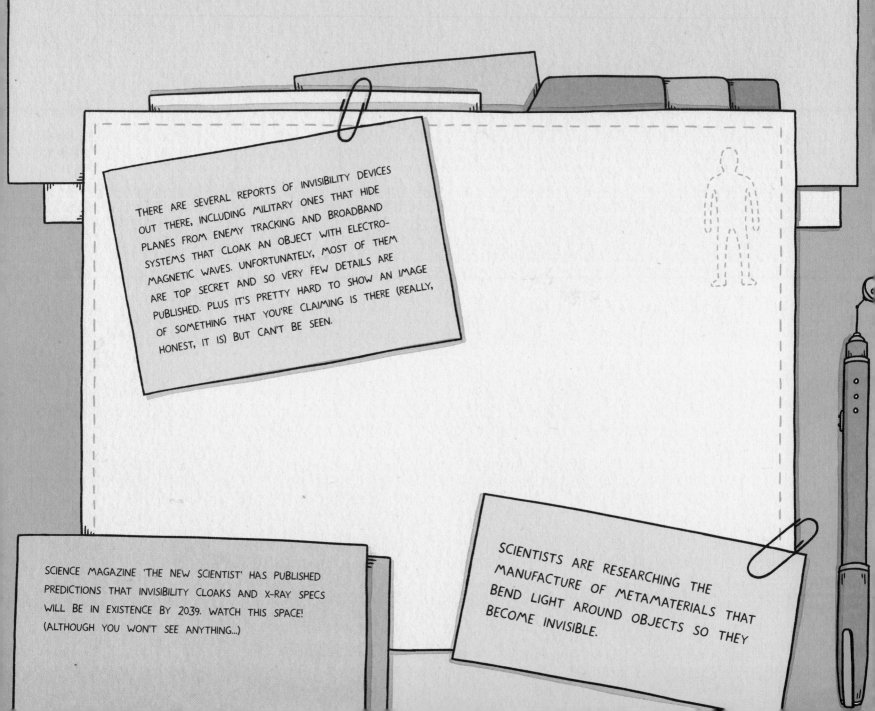

THERE ARE SEVERAL REPORTS OF INVISIBILITY DEVICES OUT THERE, INCLUDING MILITARY ONES THAT HIDE PLANES FROM ENEMY TRACKING AND BROADBAND SYSTEMS THAT CLOAK AN OBJECT WITH ELECTRO-MAGNETIC WAVES. UNFORTUNATELY, MOST OF THEM ARE TOP SECRET AND SO VERY FEW DETAILS ARE PUBLISHED. PLUS IT'S PRETTY HARD TO SHOW AN IMAGE OF SOMETHING THAT YOU'RE CLAIMING IS THERE (REALLY, HONEST, IT IS) BUT CAN'T BE SEEN.

SCIENCE MAGAZINE 'THE NEW SCIENTIST' HAS PUBLISHED PREDICTIONS THAT INVISIBILITY CLOAKS AND X-RAY SPECS WILL BE IN EXISTENCE BY 2039. WATCH THIS SPACE! (ALTHOUGH YOU WON'T SEE ANYTHING...)

SCIENTISTS ARE RESEARCHING THE MANUFACTURE OF METAMATERIALS THAT BEND LIGHT AROUND OBJECTS SO THEY BECOME INVISIBLE.

DESIGN A CAMOUFLAGE SUIT.
WHAT FEATURES WILL IT HAVE?

FEEDING TIME

IMAGINE BEING A FOOD INVENTOR
FOR A LIVING... YUM!

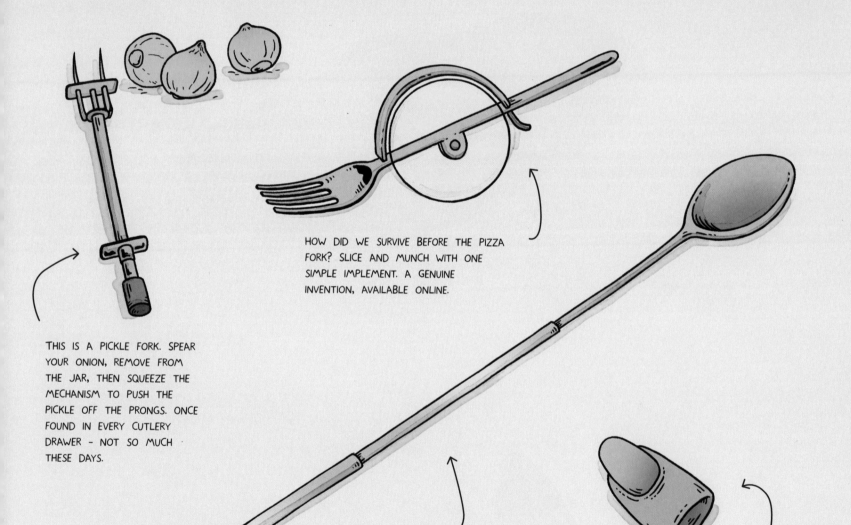

HOW DID WE SURVIVE BEFORE THE PIZZA
FORK? SLICE AND MUNCH WITH ONE
SIMPLE IMPLEMENT. A GENUINE
INVENTION, AVAILABLE ONLINE.

THIS IS A PICKLE FORK. SPEAR
YOUR ONION, REMOVE FROM
THE JAR, THEN SQUEEZE THE
MECHANISM TO PUSH THE
PICKLE OFF THE PRONGS. ONCE
FOUND IN EVERY CUTLERY
DRAWER - NOT SO MUCH
THESE DAYS.

WHILE WE'RE IN THE KITCHEN, LET'S USE AN
EXTENDABLE SPOON FOR REACHING TO THE
BOTTOM OF THE JAR. NO MORE STICKY FINGERS!

ARE YOUR THUMBS TOO WEAK? YOU NEED A
METAL THUMBNAIL, FOR PEELING THOSE PESKY
ORANGES WITH EXTRA-THICK SKIN.

CHOCOLATE-CHIP COOKIES WERE INVENTED IN 1938, WHEN RUTH WAKEFIELD USED CHUNKS OF CHOCOLATE IN A RECIPE, THINKING THEY WOULD MELT AND MAKE CHOCOLATE COOKIES. SHE GAVE THE RECIPE TO THE NESTLÉ COMPANY IN RETURN FOR A LIFETIME'S SUPPLY OF CHOCOLATE!

GEORGE CRUM, A CHEF IN NEW YORK STATE, USA, INVENTED POTATO CHIPS BY ACCIDENT. A CUSTOMER COMPLAINED HIS FRIES WERE TOO THICK, SO CRUM CUT THEM RIDICULOUSLY THIN AS A JOKE - AND THE RESULT WAS ONE OF THE BEST SNACKS EVER.

THE RECIPE FOR COCA-COLA WAS INVENTED BY A PHARMACIST, DR PEMBERTON, IN HIS BACKYARD. THE NAME AND THE DISTINCTIVE HANDWRITTEN LOGO WERE THE WORK OF HIS BOOKKEEPER.

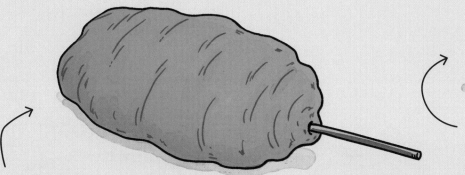

IRONICALLY, ONE OF THE MEN WHO INVENTED THE MACHINE FOR SPINNING SUPER-SUGARY COTTON CANDY WAS A DENTIST!

IN 1928, WALTER DIEMER FOUND A NEW CHEWING GUM FORMULA THAT WAS MORE FLEXIBLE AND LESS STICKY, ALLOWING THE CHEWER TO BLOW BUBBLES. IT WAS SOLD AS 'DUBBLE BUBBLE'. SALES PEOPLE HAD TO BE TAUGHT HOW TO BLOW BUBBLES WITH IT, SO THEY COULD DEMONSTRATE IT TO THEIR CUSTOMERS.

SNACK ATTACK

DESIGN SOME AWESOME NEW SNACKS
TO KEEP RUMBLY TUMMIES AT BAY!

SWEET TREATS

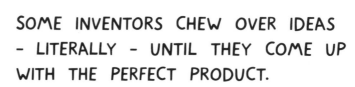

SOME INVENTORS CHEW OVER IDEAS - LITERALLY - UNTIL THEY COME UP WITH THE PERFECT PRODUCT.

US INVENTOR THOMAS ADAMS WAS DETERMINED THAT NATURAL GUM (CHICLE) COULD BE MADE INTO SOMETHING USEFUL. HE TRIED TURNING IT INTO TOYS, BOOTS, TIRES, AND MASKS BEFORE POPPING A PIECE INTO HIS MOUTH AND REALIZING THAT IT TASTED OKAY. HE HAD THE IDEA OF ADDING DIFFERENT FLAVORS, AND OPENED THE WORLD'S FIRST CHEWING GUM FACTORY. HIS 'NEW YORK GUM' WENT ON SALE IN 1871.

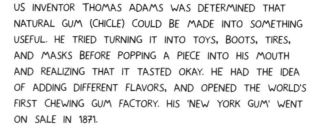

INVENT A BRAND-NEW CANDY
TO SHARE WITH THE WORLD!

STRETCH YOUR BRAIN AND SEE IF YOU CAN INVENT
SOMETHING REALLY FUN. HOW ABOUT A FOOD-TASTING MACHINE?
OR A DEVICE FOR TIGHTROPE PRACTICE?

WHATEVER FLOATS YOUR BOAT...

WATER VEHICLES DATE BACK OVER 8,000 YEARS, WHEN THE ANCIENT EGYPTIANS BUILT BOATS OUT OF REEDS.

DID YOU KNOW? THE ONLY US PRESIDENT TO HOLD A PATENT IS ABRAHAM LINCOLN (1809-65) FOR A DEVICE TO LIFT BOATS OVER BLOCKAGES, ALTHOUGH HIS INVENTION WAS NEVER ACTUALLY PRODUCED AND SOLD.

CHRISTOPHER COCKERELL, INVENTOR OF THE HOVERCRAFT, TESTED HIS IDEAS FOR A BOAT THAT MOVED ON A CUSHION OF AIR AT HOME USING TWO TIN CANS AND A VACUUM CLEANER.

THE WORLD'S LARGEST PASSENGER SHIPS WERE LAUNCHED IN 2009 AND 2010 RESPECTIVELY. THE 'OASIS CLASS' CRUISE LINERS CARRY OVER 5,400 PASSENGERS, AND HAVE ON-BOARD GYMS, CLIMBING WALLS, PARKS, THEATERS, MOVIE THEATERS, AND EVEN A ZIP WIRE!

ITALIAN COMPANY SBK ENGINEERING HAS INVENTED THE 'SHUTTLE BIKE' - TWO INFLATABLE FLOATS THAT CAN BE CARRIED IN A BACKPACK AND THEN ATTACHED TO YOUR ROAD BIKE IF YOU HAPPEN TO RUN OUT OF ROAD.

KEEP THIS MAN AFLOAT WITH AN
AMAZING INVENTION OF YOUR OWN.

SEA-SHOES

YES - YOU READ THAT RIGHT.
SEA-SHOES. SOMEONE ALREADY
INVENTED THEM.

INVENTOR M.W. HULTON'S 1960S SEA-SHOES NOT
ONLY SEE YOU SAFE AND DRY ACROSS THE
WATER, THEY ALSO COME WITH POLES (FOR
BALANCE, OBV) AND DUCKFOOT PROPELLERS
ON THE BACK TO MOVE THINGS ALONG. NOPE,
NO IDEA WHAT THESE ARE, BUT THEY SOUND
AMAZING. AND FLAPPY.

SNOW RIDE

THERE'S NO BUSINESS LIKE SNOW BUSINESS...

AS THE SAYING GOES, NECESSITY IS THE MOTHER OF INVENTION. WHICH IS WHY IT WAS ALWAYS MORE LIKELY THAT THE SNOWMOBILE WOULD BE INVENTED IN CANADA THAN IN SINGAPORE, SAY. IT TOOK A WANNABE MECHANIC FROM QUEBEC NAMED JOSEPH-ARMAND BOMBARDIER TO DEVISE A WAY TO BUILD A VEHICLE THAT COULD SUCCESSFULLY BE DRIVEN ACROSS SNOW AND ICE. HIS FIRST SNOWMOBILE, INVENTED IN 1922 WHEN HE WAS JUST 15 YEARS OLD, USED A CAR ENGINE AND A PROPELLER TO MOVE IT ACROSS THE SNOW.

I WONDER WHETHER BOMBARDIER WOULD RECOGNIZE THE MODERN SNOWMOBILE!

THE 'MUSKEG' ALL-TERRAIN TRACTOR WAS ALSO BOMBARDIER'S INVENTION. IT CAN BE DRIVEN ON SNOW BUT ALSO IN BOGGY, SWAMPY AREAS AND ON SAND.

STRAP ON SOME SKIS AND
INVENT A SNOW-RIDING DEVICE!

FLIGHTS OF FANCY

HERE'S ONE OF THOSE 'IN YOUR DREAMS'
MOMENTS FROM INVENTING HISTORY.

KENT COUCH OF OREGON, USA, SOARS HIGH IN
THE SKY ON A DECKCHAIR ATTACHED TO OVER
100 LARGE HELIUM BALLOONS. HE HAS
INSTRUMENTS TO TELL HIM HOW HIGH HE IS,
WHERE HE IS, AND HOW FAST HE IS GOING.

ON ONE FLIGHT, HE SHOT THE BALLOONS WITH
BALL BEARINGS TO BRING HIS CHAIR DOWN TO
LAND. HE LATER DEVELOPED A WAY TO LET
HELIUM OUT TO GIVE HIM A MORE CONTROLLED
DESCENT. BY 2012, KENT HAD FIGURED OUT HOW
TO TAKE ALONG A CO-PILOT, WHEN HE AND
CAPTAIN FAREED LAFTA REACHED OVER 14,000
FEET.

- TOTAL DISTANCE (TRIP 1): 240 MILES
- AVERAGE SPEED: 22 MPH
- MAXIMUM HEIGHT: 14,000 FEET
- SNACKS FOR THE JOURNEY: BEEF JERKY,
  BOILED EGGS, CHOCOLATE, AND COFFEE
- DOWNSIDE: US$1500 FINE FOR VIOLATING
  AIR TRAFFIC RULES

HOW WOULD YOU USE HOT AIR TO TRAVEL?

INVENT A WRITING TOOL THAT
ALL YOUR FRIENDS WOULD USE.

QUICK ON THE DRAW

NOW HERE'S AN INVENTION TO DRAW EVERYONE'S ATTENTION - THE COOLEST CRAYONS YOU CAN IMAGINE.

CRAYOLA CRAYONS WERE INVENTED BY TWO COUSINS: EDWIN BINNEY AND C. HAROLD SMITH. THEY HAD ALREADY COME UP WITH A WAX CRAYON THAT WAS USED TO WRITE ON BARRELS AND CRATES, BUT IT CONTAINED TOXIC SUBSTANCES. SO THE SEARCH WAS ON TO FIND A RECIPE THAT COULD BE USED TO MAKE SAFE DRAWING STICKS FOR KIDS, WHICH COULD BE PRODUCED IN LOTS OF DIFFERENT COLORS. CRAYOLA CRAYONS EMERGED IN 1903, NAMED BY BINNEY'S WIFE FROM THE FRENCH WORD FOR CHALK, 'CRAIE', PLUS THE WORD 'OILY'.

CRAYONS HAVE GONE FROM STRENGTH TO STRENGTH AND NOW THERE ARE LOTS OF DIFFERENT TYPES. THERE ARE ONES THAT SMELL LIKE FLOWERS, ONES THAT GLOW IN THE DARK AND CHANGE COLOR, NOT TO MENTION GLITTERY ONES, METALLIC ONES, NEON ONES, TRIANGULAR ONES, AND WASHABLE ONES. SOMEONE OUGHT TO INVENT EDIBLE ONES.

THE IMPORTANCE OF BEING USELESS

THE JAPANESE HAVE A SPECIAL WORD IN THEIR LANGUAGE FOR 'THE ART OF DESIGNING BIZARRE, PURPOSELESS INVENTIONS': 'CHINDOGU'. THIS ART, IN TURN, HAS COINED A NEW ENGLISH WORD: 'UNUSELESS' - THAT'S TO SAY, CHINDOGU AREN'T ACTUALLY USELESS, BECAUSE THEY ALWAYS AIM TO SOLVE A PROBLEM, BUT THEY CAN'T REALLY BE DESCRIBED AS USEFUL.

CHINDOGU HAVE CERTAIN RULES, SUCH AS THE FACT THAT THEY MUST BE MADE, NOT JUST EXIST AS DRAWINGS AND PLANS. THEY'RE NOT ALLOWED TO BE PATENTED, HOWEVER. SO WHAT ARE YOU WAITING FOR?! THESE EXAMPLES MAY INSPIRE YOU...

THESE ATTRACTIVE GOLD EARRINGS WOULD BE HANDY FOR A VERY LOUD PARTY AS THEY COME WITH EARPLUGS!

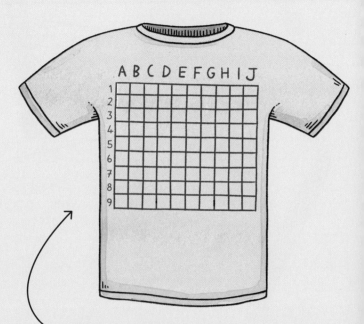

DUSTER SLIPPERS FOR CATS SO THAT THEY CLEAN YOUR FLOOR AS THEY WALK. THANKS, PUSS!

AND THE BACKSCRATCHER T-SHIRT, SO YOU CAN PINPOINT EXACTLY WHERE YOUR ITCH NEEDS TO BE SCRATCHED. I WANT ONE.

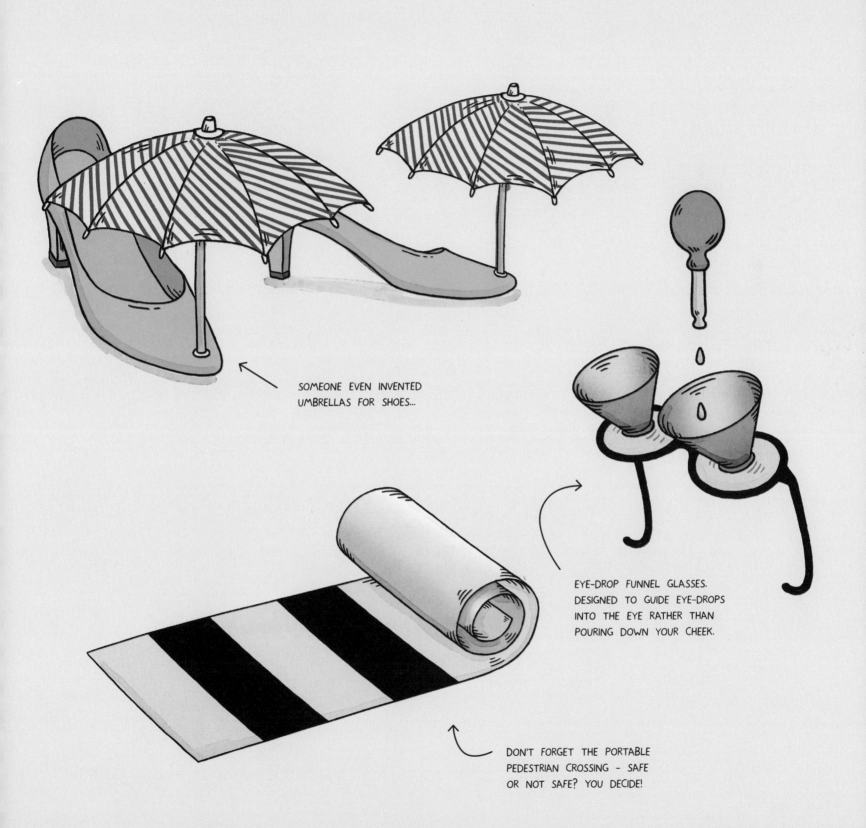

SOMEONE EVEN INVENTED
UMBRELLAS FOR SHOES...

EYE-DROP FUNNEL GLASSES.
DESIGNED TO GUIDE EYE-DROPS
INTO THE EYE RATHER THAN
POURING DOWN YOUR CHEEK.

DON'T FORGET THE PORTABLE
PEDESTRIAN CROSSING - SAFE
OR NOT SAFE? YOU DECIDE!

NOW HERE'S SOMETHING THAT COULD MAKE YOU VERY POPULAR INDEED - CAN YOU INVENT SOMETHING THAT WOULD HELP YOU WITH YOUR HOMEWORK?

TEDDIES IN SPACE

LET'S START WITH SOMETHING THAT IS LITERALLY OUT OF THIS WORLD. ASTRO-TEDDIES!

PLASTIC BOTTLE HELMET

TINFOIL SUIT

PLASTIC BOTTLE PROTECTION

BOX CONTAINING CAMERAS, EQUIPMENT, ETC.

A GROUP OF SCHOOLCHILDREN FROM CAMBRIDGE, UK, SUCCESSFULLY SENT FOUR SOFT TOYS INTO SPACE FOR THEIR SCIENCE PROJECT. THE TEDDIES WERE LAUNCHED USING A HELIUM WEATHER BALLOON, AND TRAVELED STRAPPED ALONGSIDE A FOAM-PADDED BOX CONTAINING A WEBCAM, RADIO TRANSMITTER, AND PARACHUTE FOR THEIR LANDING. TEMPERATURE SENSORS WERE TAPED TO THE TEDDIES' CHESTS, AND RECORDED FREEZING CONDITIONS OF -63°F, BUT THE BOLD BEARS WERE PROTECTED BY SPECIAL SPACESUITS DESIGNED BY THE STUDENTS. THEIR JOURNEY LASTED OVER TWO HOURS AND REACHED HEIGHTS OF OVER 18.6 MILES.

THE FIRST JOURNEYS INTO SPACE WERE TOO
DANGEROUS FOR HUMANS - SCIENTISTS COULDN'T
GUARANTEE THAT WHAT WENT UP WOULD COME
BACK DOWN (ALIVE). IN THE 1940S AND 50S,
SEVERAL MONKEYS WERE LAUNCHED IN
EXPERIMENTAL FLIGHTS.

THE FIRST ORBITING SPACECRAFT WAS
SPUTNIK 1 IN 1957. THAT SAME YEAR,
SPUTNIK 2 CARRIED A DOG CALLED LAIKA
INTO ORBIT. ONLY FOUR YEARS LATER,
THE FIRST HUMAN, YURI GAGARIN, WAS
SUCCESSFULLY SENT INTO ORBIT - AND, MOST
IMPORTANTLY, BROUGHT SAFELY BACK AGAIN.

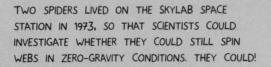

TWO SPIDERS LIVED ON THE SKYLAB SPACE
STATION IN 1973, SO THAT SCIENTISTS COULD
INVESTIGATE WHETHER THEY COULD STILL SPIN
WEBS IN ZERO-GRAVITY CONDITIONS. THEY COULD!

WHAT WOULD YOU SEND
INTO SPACE AND
HOW WOULD IT GET
BACK DOWN?

ANYONE NEED A RIDE?

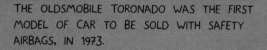

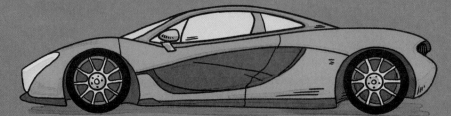

THE OLDSMOBILE TORONADO WAS THE FIRST MODEL OF CAR TO BE SOLD WITH SAFETY AIRBAGS, IN 1973.

AT LEAST 100,000 PATENTED IDEAS HAVE CONTRIBUTED TO THE CREATION OF THE MOTOR CAR.

WINDSHIELD WIPERS WERE INVENTED IN 1903. IN THE US, MARY ANDERSON FILED A PATENT FOR HER 'WINDOW CLEANING DEVICE' THAT WAS OPERATED BY A LEVER INSIDE THE CAR. IRISH INVENTOR JAMES HENRY APJOHN PATENTED HIS VERSION IN THE UK - TWO BRUSHES THAT COULD BE MOVED OVER THE WINDSHIELD.

CRUISE CONTROL FOR CARS WAS INVENTED BY RALPH TEETOR, A PROLIFIC AMERICAN INVENTOR WHO WAS BLIND FROM THE AGE OF FIVE.

THE 'DRIVESUIT' IS A HANDMADE TRANSFORMER COSTUME THAT ALLOWS THE WEARER TO WALK AROUND LIKE A ROBOT, OR DRIVE ALONG ON ALL FOURS USING THE MOTORIZED DRIVE BOOTS WITH WHEELS ATTACHED. CREATED BY DREW BEAUMIER, THE SUITS COST AROUND US$1800 EACH.

FLYING CAR

TERRAFUGIA, AN AMERICAN COMPANY, HAS DEVELOPED THE 'TRANSITION' FLYING CAR. THE FIRST PROTOTYPE FLEW IN 2012 AND CARRIES A SINGLE PILOT AT A FLIGHT CRUISING SPEED OF AROUND 100 MPH. WHEN IT'S TIME TO LAND, JUST TOUCH DOWN AT YOUR NEAREST AIRPORT, FOLD UP THE WINGS, AND YOU'RE READY TO HIT THE ROAD. THE AIRCRAFT IS EVEN TINY ENOUGH TO FIT INTO YOUR GARAGE AT HOME! ONE SMALL PROBLEM, THOUGH - ONLY TWO HAVE BEEN MADE, AT A COST OF AROUND US$280,000 EACH!

DESIGN YOUR OWN VEHICLE THAT DOES TWO JOBS IN ONE.

WHAT CAR ACCESSORIES
WOULD YOU INVENT?

CRAZY CAR

EVERYONE NEEDS A COOL SET OF WHEELS
BUT THESE ARE TOTALLY HOT!

THE FIRST CAR RADIO WAS INVENTED IN CHICAGO
IN 1930. IT WAS ONE OF THE FIRST PRODUCTS
TO BE MADE BY THE MOTOROLA COMPANY, WHO
ALSO PIONEERED MOBILE CELLULAR PHONES.

IT'S ONLY A CAR WITH FLAME THROWERS ON
THE SIDES! INVENTED TO PROTECT DRIVERS FROM
CAR CRIMES - BUT CONTROVERSIAL AND NO
LONGER ON SALE - THIS CAR STORES LIQUIFIED
GAS IN THE BACK WHICH IS THEN SQUIRTED OUT
THROUGH NOZZLES UNDER THE FRONT DOORS.
STAY AWAY, CARJACKERS!

DRAW YOUR DREAM CAR.

CUSTOMIZE YOUR BIKE!

ON YOUR BIKE

INVENTING A SINGLE-USE VEHICLE OBVIOUSLY ISN'T ENOUGH THESE DAYS – DUAL-PURPOSE IS THE WAY TO GO.

HERE'S ANOTHER ONE. KEEP PEDALING AND SOON YOU'LL BE PADDLING! IT'S A FLOATING BICYCLE WITH CATAMARAN HULLS, AND A PROPELLER THAT IS TURNED BY MOVING THE PEDALS. ONE SUCH CONTRAPTION WAS BUILT IN 1914 BY H.G. BELBIN OF LONDON.

HERE'S A BIKE. HONESTLY, IT IS. IT'S JUST THAT IT HAS FLOATING GLOBES INSTEAD OF WHEELS. OF COURSE. IT WAS INVENTED IN THE 1930S BY A FRENCHMAN AND DEMONSTRATED IN A LARGE SWIMMING POOL. SMALL FINS ON THE BACK 'WHEEL' MOVE IT THROUGH THE WATER, AND THE SMALL FLOATS CAN MOVE DOWN TO PROVIDE BALANCE WHILE AFLOAT.

WHAT WOULD YOUR
UNICYCLE LOOK LIKE?

ON ONE WHEEL

WHO KNOWS - MAYBE IN
THE ECO-FRIENDLY FUTURE,
WHEELS WILL BE RATIONED?

THE 'MONOWHEEL' DIFFERS FROM A
UNICYCLE IN THE POSITION OF ITS
RIDER, WHO SITS INSIDE THE WHEEL
RATHER THAN PERCHED ON TOP. WHICH
MAKES SOME SENSE - IT JUST LOOKS
ODD. THE FIRST MONOWHEEL WAS BUILT IN
FRANCE IN 1869 AND FOR DECADES
INVENTORS TRIED TO DEVELOP IT AS A
SERIOUS FORM OF TRANSPORT.

TIME FOR BED

EVEN INVENTORS NEED SOME SLEEP.

MATTHEW GALE HAS DESIGNED A COAT THAT LETS YOU SLEEP ANYTIME, ANY PLACE, ANYWHERE. THE 'EXCUBO' JACKET HAS AN EXTRA HIGH, STIFF COLLAR THAT SUPPORTS YOUR HEAD AS YOU SNOOZE IN A SITTING POSITION. SLIP ON YOUR SHADES AND NO ONE WILL KNOW THAT YOU'RE IN THE LAND OF NOD (UNLESS YOU SNORE OR DRIBBLE).

WEAR THE PHILIP STEIN SLEEP BRACELET TO BED AND IT'S SAID IT WILL ENCOURAGE YOUR BODY TO PRODUCE MORE MELATONIN, WHICH IS THE HORMONE THAT HELPS YOU SLEEP. UNFORTUNATELY, THE PRODUCT HAS A NIGHTMARISH US$395 PRICE TAG!

IF YOU CAN'T DRIFT OFF WITHOUT SOMEONE GIVING
YOU A CUDDLE, THIS PILLOW WILL HELP. IT'S DESIGNED
IN THE SHAPE OF A PERSON, WITH A SOFT CHEST TO
SNUGGLE INTO, AND A COMFORTING ARM TO WRAP
AROUND YOU. ZZZZZZ.

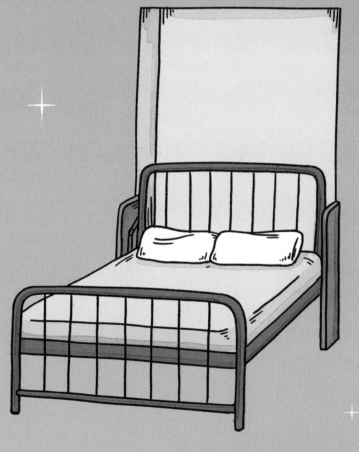

THE 'DISAPPEARING BED' WAS PATENTED IN 1912 BY WILLIAM
MURPHY. IT FOLDED AWAY INTO THE WALL TO LEAVE MORE
ROOM SPACE. STILL USED TODAY, THEY ARE OFTEN CALLED
MURPHY BEDS, ESPECIALLY IN THE USA.

WAKEY-WAKEY!

SO, NOW YOU KNOW HOW TO SNOOZE,
IT'S TIME TO GET UP!

THE 'CLOCKY' ALARM IS A TINY ROBOT ON WHEELS
THAT RUNS AWAY, BEEPING LOUDLY, SO YOU HAVE TO
JUMP OUT OF BED AND CATCH IT TO TURN IT OFF.
NOW YOU'RE WIDE AWAKE!

WE'RE NOT TELLING PORKIES - SOMEONE HAS
DREAMED UP AN ALARM CLOCK THAT COOKS
BREAKFAST BY YOUR BED! THE 'WAKE 'N' BACON'
WORKS BY WAKING YOU WITH THE AROMA OF
SIZZLING RASHERS - ALLEGEDLY.

MAKE SURE THIS GADGET
COVERS ALL OF YOUR
MORNING REQUIREMENTS.

WHEN NATURE CALLS

SOMETIMES IT'S WHERE WE HAVE OUR BEST IDEAS...

TOILETS ON THE INTERNATIONAL SPACE
STATION (AND PLANES) USE AIR
INSTEAD OF WATER FOR FLUSHING.
AND IN SPACE, THE ASTRONAUTS' PEE
IS RECYCLED INTO DRINKING WATER!

I BELIEVE I CAN FLY

LEONARDO DA VINCI STUDIED BIRD FLIGHT TO TRY
TO INVENT A FLYING MACHINE. AROUND 1485 HE
DREW UP A DESIGN THAT INVOLVED LYING ON A
PLANK AND USING PULLEYS, LEVERS AND PEDALS
TO FLAP TWO LARGE WINGS.

THE WRIGHT BROTHERS, AMERICAN PIONEERS OF THE
AIRPLANE, WERE INSPIRED IN THEIR RESEARCH BY A TOY
PLANE GIVEN TO THEM BY THEIR FATHER, WHICH WAS
POWERED BY TWISTING A RUBBER BAND.

ONE COMPANY HAS INVENTED AN UNMANNED FLYING DRONE
CALLED THE 'TACOCOPTER' TO DELIVER FAST FOOD STRAIGHT
TO YOUR DOOR. IT ISN'T IN PRODUCTION YET (OR LEGAL).

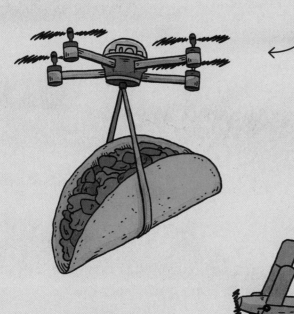

AMPHIBIOUS HELICOPTERS - WHICH CAN LAND ON
(AND TAKE OFF FROM) BOTH LAND AND WATER
- FIRST APPEARED IN 1941.

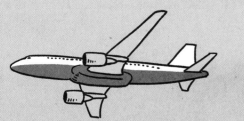

IN 1876 A FRENCHMAN, ALPHONSE PÉNAUD, FILED
THE FIRST PATENT FOR A FLYING MACHINE THAT
COULD TRAVEL ON WATER. CAN YOU SEE ITS
BOAT-SHAPED HULL?

HOW WOULD YOU TAKE
TO THE SKIES?

THE 'FLYING PLATFORM' WAS DEVELOPED IN THE 1950S FOR THE US ARMY, BUT
WAS DEEMED UNPRACTICAL FOR USE IN COMBAT. IT'S NOT HARD TO SEE WHY...

'JETMAN' (AKA YVES ROSSY FROM SWITZERLAND) SOARS THROUGH THE AIR USING HIS WONDROUS INVENTION: A PERSONAL JETPACK WITH WINGS. HE USED IT TO FLY AROUND MOUNT FUJI IN JAPAN IN 2013, FREE AS A BIRD AND TOTALLY AT ONE WITH THE SKIES.

ROCKET MAN

IS IT POSSIBLE FOR HUMANS TO FLY WITHOUT A PLANE? OF COURSE IT IS. FORGET YOUR HANG-GLIDERS AND MICROLIGHTS - CHECK THESE OUT.

THE 'JETLEV' STAYS A LITTLE CLOSER TO HOME, BUT STILL ROCKETS THE WEARER 30 FEET INTO THE SKIES - USING WATER POWER. INVENTED IN FLORIDA IN 2012, THE 'JETLEV' IS ATTACHED TO A SMALL BOAT-SHAPED POD BY A WATER HOSE THAT PROVIDES THE THRUST TO SEND YOU SOARING UP AND AWAY AT SPEEDS OF AROUND 25 MPH.

SKY CYCLE

IS IT A PLANE?
IS IT A TRICYCLE?
YES, IT'S BOTH!

TRAFFIC JAMS BEGONE! US INVENTOR LARRY NEAL HAS DREAMED UP A WAY OF LEAVING THE TRAFFIC BEHIND AND TAKING TO THE SKIES. HIS 'SUPER SKY CYCLE' CAN BE DRIVEN ALONG A NORMAL ROAD AT SPEEDS OF UP TO 55 MPH. BUT IF THE TRAFFIC COMES TO A STANDSTILL, IT HAS ROTORS WHICH OPEN UP AND LIFT IT INTO THE AIR.

THERE IS ONE SMALL PROBLEM - TO GET ENOUGH LIFT FROM THE ROTORS, YOU NEED TO BE MOVING ALONG THE GROUND AT SPEED - WHICH YOU JUST CAN'T DO IN A TRAFFIC JAM! BACK TO THE DRAWING BOARD FOR THAT ONE. BUT IT'S STILL A MIGHTY COOL MACHINE.

WHAT ARE THESE ROTORS
KEEPING UP IN THE AIR?

FROM SEA TO SKY

YET AGAIN, WE HAVE LIFT-OFF!

THE 'FLYING HOVERCRAFT' USES THE 'WIG' EFFECT
(THIS STANDS FOR 'WING IN GROUND' – LOOK IT
UP!), MOVING ALONG THE GROUND AS NORMAL
UNTIL IT REACHES 44 MPH WHEN IT TAKES OFF
AND FLIES AT EVEN FASTER SPEEDS. IT HAS ROOM
FOR A DRIVER AND A PASSENGER, AND WAS
MADE FROM ALL SORTS OF THINGS, INCLUDING
THE GAS BOTTLE FROM A BARBECUE, BY NEW
ZEALAND MECHANIC RUDY HEEMAN.

HOW WOULD YOU MAKE
THIS BOAT FLY?

OH NO! THE CAR ON THIS PAGE HAS
BEEN SHRUNK TO THE SIZE OF A PEA!

DRAW THE INCREDIBLE SHRINKING MACHINE THAT DID IT.

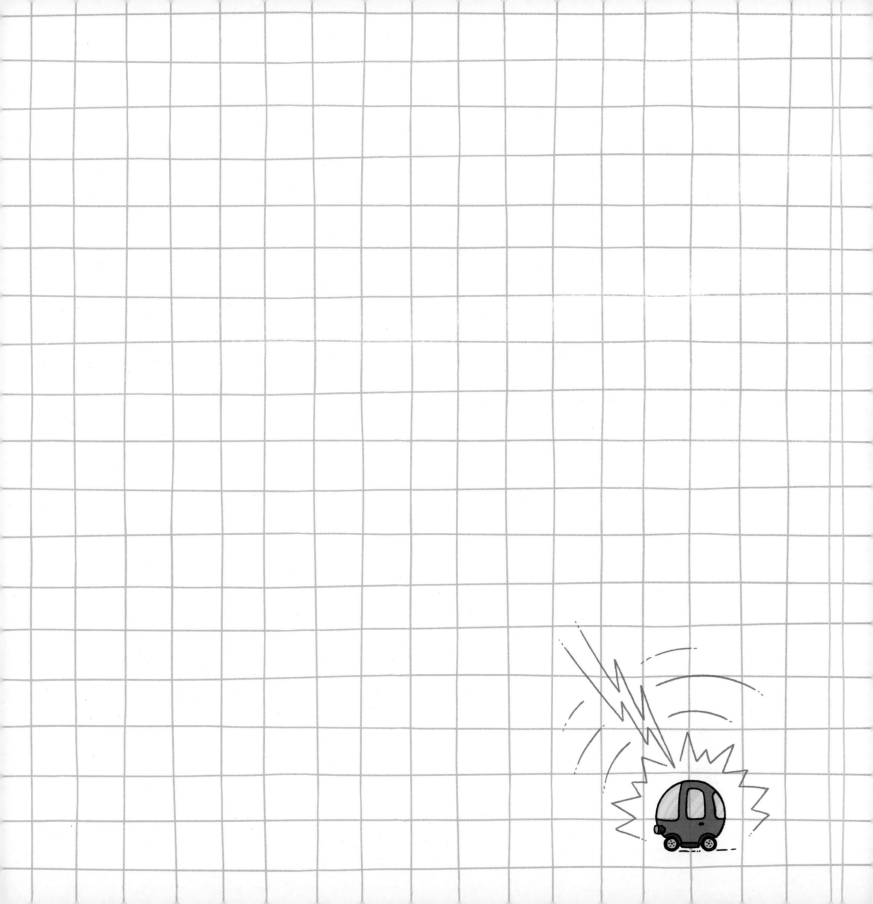

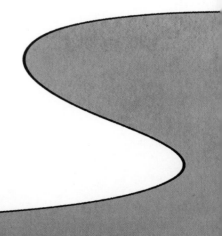

THE QUICKEST WAY TO TRAVEL AROUND THE
WORLD IS BY JET PLANE, AND THAT STILL
TAKES OVER TWO DAYS.

CAN YOU INVENT A
FASTER METHOD OF VISITING
FRIENDS THAT LIVE FAR AWAY?

INVENT A TOY... JUST FOR FUN

PLAY TIME

DON'T FALL INTO THE TRAP OF THINKING THAT ALL INVENTIONS HAVE TO CHANGE THE WORLD. FUN, GAMES, AND HOME IMPROVEMENTS ALL PLAY AN IMPORTANT PART IN OUR DAILY LIVES.

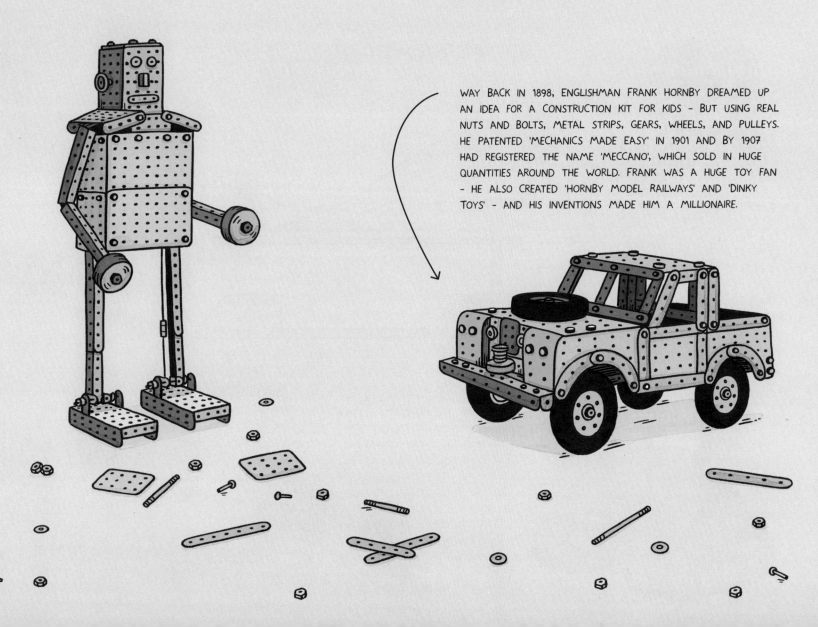

WAY BACK IN 1898, ENGLISHMAN FRANK HORNBY DREAMED UP AN IDEA FOR A CONSTRUCTION KIT FOR KIDS - BUT USING REAL NUTS AND BOLTS, METAL STRIPS, GEARS, WHEELS, AND PULLEYS. HE PATENTED 'MECHANICS MADE EASY' IN 1901 AND BY 1907 HAD REGISTERED THE NAME 'MECCANO', WHICH SOLD IN HUGE QUANTITIES AROUND THE WORLD. FRANK WAS A HUGE TOY FAN - HE ALSO CREATED 'HORNBY MODEL RAILWAYS' AND 'DINKY TOYS' - AND HIS INVENTIONS MADE HIM A MILLIONAIRE.

MEGA CHAIR

THE 'HOVERIT' LOUNGER IS A NEW CONCEPT IN COMFORT... IT FLOATS!
USING THE REPELLING FORCES OF MAGNETS - IN MUCH THE SAME WAY
AS A 'MAGLEV' TRAIN - THE CHAIR IS ALMOST SUSPENDED IN MID-AIR.
IT MOVES AND WOBBLES AS YOU SETTLE DOWN FOR SOME SERIOUS
RESTING. THE ONLY FIXED PARTS ARE TWO POLES BY THE ARMRESTS,
WHICH PREVENT THE CHAIR FROM FLOATING OFF AND TIPPING YOU ON
TO THE FLOOR. IT'S SOMETHING OF A COLLECTOR'S ITEM AS ONLY 2,000
WERE MADE - AND DON'T POSITION IT TOO CLOSE TO THE KITCHEN OR
YOU MIGHT FIND YOURSELF THE TARGET OF FLYING FORKS, KNIVES, AND
OTHER METALLIC OBJECTS. NOT SO RELAXING AFTER ALL...

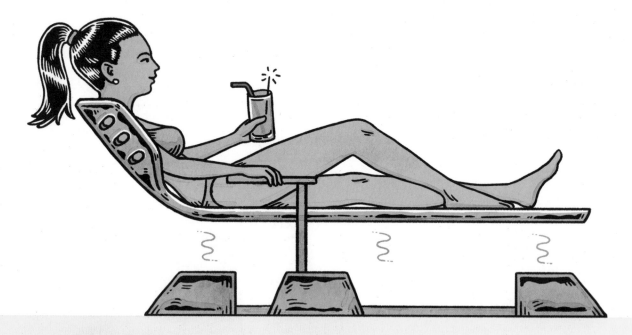

IF YOU'RE FEELING RESTLESS, THEN MAYBE THE
'TANKCHAIR' IS MORE YOUR SCENE? CUSHIONED,
COMFORTABLE, AND ALL-TERRAIN FOR WHEN YOU
NEED TO TACKLE STEEP SLOPES AND MUDDY
PUDDLES - IT EVEN PLOUGHS THROUGH SNOW!
JOKING ASIDE, IT WAS ACTUALLY INVENTED FOR
WHEELCHAIR USERS WHO WANT TO HEAD FOR THE
GREAT OUTDOORS, AND WAS THE BRAINCHILD OF
EX-US SOLDIER BRAD SODEN, WHO DESIGNED IT
FOR HIS WIFE.

ADD SOME EXTRAS TO MAKE
THIS CHAIR THE MOST RELAXING EVER.

DO YOU FIND SITTING STILL QUITE BORING?
THEN INVENT A CHAIR THAT MOVES AROUND!

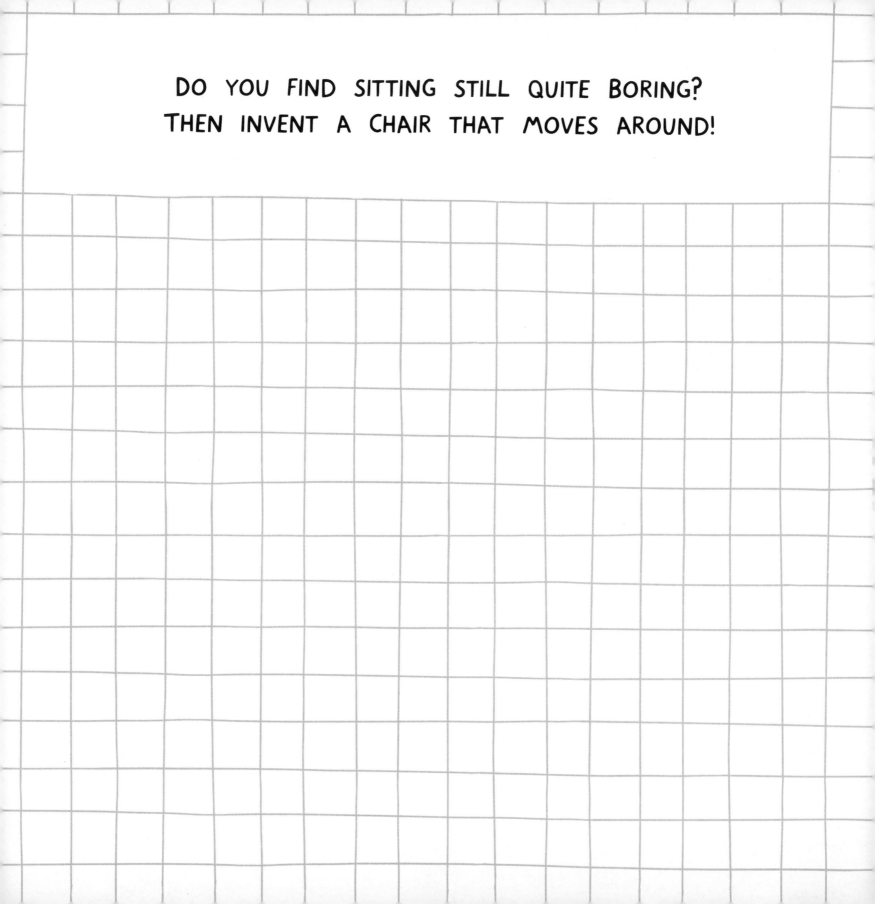

BE A GOOD SPORT

PRACTICE MAKES PERFECT, EH?

THIS MACHINE MIGHT LOOK LIKE A MEDIEVAL TORTURE DEVICE, BUT IT'S NOT. IT'S A TOTALLY MODERN APPROACH TO GETTING THE PERFECT GOLF SWING. IT MAY NOT SOLVE GLOBAL PROBLEMS OR SAVE LIVES, BUT IT'S GREAT FOR HELPING YOU TO HIT THAT PESKY LITTLE BALL PROPERLY. AND ITS NAME IS GOOD: THE 'SURE SWING GOLF THING'. OH - SORRY - IT'S ACTUALLY JUST THE 'SURE SWING'. GAH.

MANY SPORTS JUST KIND OF HAPPENED AND EVOLVED, WAY BACK IN TIME, BUT BASKETBALL WAS ACTUALLY, PROPERLY INVENTED. SPORTS TEACHER DR JAMES NAISMITH USED PEACH BASKETS AND A SOCCER BALL TO HELP KEEP HIS STUDENTS FIT INDOORS DURING THE WINTER OF 1891.

VOLLEYBALL WAS INVENTED IN 1895 BY WILLIAM MORGAN, BUT WAS ORIGINALLY CALLED 'MINTONETTE' BECAUSE OF ITS SIMILARITIES TO BADMINTON.

SOCCER HAS BEEN PLAYED FOR THOUSANDS OF YEARS. LINEN BALLS WERE EVEN FOUND IN ANCIENT EGYPTIAN TOMBS. EARLY BALLS WERE MADE FROM INFLATED PIGS' BLADDERS.

EIGHTEEN-YEAR-OLD RALPH SAMUELSON INVENTED THE SPORT OF WATERSKIING IN 1922, USING WOOD FROM BARRELS AND SNOW SKIS ON WATER. BUT HE FAILED TO PATENT THEM! THE FIRST PATENT FOR WATERSKIS WAS IN 1925.

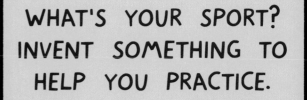

DINOSAURS BROUGHT TO LIFE

IN SCARY ROBOT FORM - YIKES!

THE MOVIE 'JURASSIC PARK' WAS ONE OF THE FIRST TO COMBINE ANIMATRONICS (LIFELIKE ROBOTS) AND EARLY CGI (COMPUTER-GENERATED IMAGERY) AND AMAZED AUDIENCES IN 1993.

THINK OF A TRANSFORMER THAT TURNS INTO A DINOSAUR INSTEAD OF A CAR. NOW IMAGINE IT PICKING UP VEHICLES AND EATING THEM, SNATCHING UP SMALL PLANES AND CRUSHING THEM, AND BREATHING FIRE. SCARY STUFF! 'ROBOSAURUS' DOES ALL OF THESE THINGS, WITH HYDRAULIC ARMS, GRASPING CLAWS, AND A FLAME THROWER IN ITS HEAD. INVENTED BY DOUG MALEWICKI IN 1989, THE MONSTER COST US$2.2 MILLION TO BUILD, AND HAS INSPIRED VARIOUS IMITATORS SUCH AS 'MEGASAURUS' AND 'TRANSAURUS'.

- MAXIMUM HEIGHT 40 FEET

- WEIGHS OVER 30 TONS

- AIR CANNONS FIRE MISSILES, CONFETTI AND FIREWORKS

- TRANSFORMS FROM TRAVEL MODE IN UNDER TWO MINUTES

- CONTROLLED BY PILOT INSIDE ROBOT HEAD

- FLAMES SHOOT 20 FEET

- MOVES USING 18 SEPARATE HYDRAULIC SYSTEMS

BEST FOOT FORWARD

ONCE UPON A TIME, THERE WAS NO SUCH
THING AS SNEAKERS - IMAGINE THAT!

SHOES DESIGNED SPECIFICALLY FOR SPORTS WERE
MADE IN THE FIRST HALF OF THE 19TH CENTURY,
WHEN CHARLES GOODYEAR INVENTED VULCANIZED
RUBBER THAT WAS STRONG AND FLEXIBLE AND
COULD BE MOLDED TO MAKE THE SOLES OF SHOES.

MODERN SNEAKERS USE ALL SORTS OF TECHNOLOGY TO
INCREASE COMFORT AND PERFORMANCE. SOME PUMP AIR
INTO THE SHOES TO GIVE A BETTER FIT, WHILE OTHERS
USE POCKETS OF GAS TO CUSHION YOUR STEP. ONE
COMPANY HAS PUT SPRINGS IN THE SOLES TO REDUCE
STRESS ON THE BONES IN YOUR FEET.

CUSTOMIZE THIS SHOE FOR MAXIMUM PERFORMANCE
- OR JUST MAXIMUM STYLE.

ROUND AND ROUND

THE FIRST EVER FERRIS WHEEL WAS INVENTED BY AMERICAN ENGINEER GEORGE WASHINGTON GALE FERRIS JR (BIG NAME, BIG IDEAS...) FOR THE CHICAGO WORLD'S FAIR IN 1893. IT WAS DESIGNED TO BE EVEN MORE STUPENDOUS THAN THE EIFFEL TOWER, WHICH HAD BEEN BUILT FOR THE PARIS WORLD'S FAIR OF 1889.

THINK OF A NEW KIND
OF FAIRGROUND RIDE THAT
WILL BLOW YOUR MIND!

HAVE YOU EVER COME UP WITH AN AMAZING IDEA JUST BY LYING ON THE
GRASS, GAZING INTO THE SUMMER SKY? THAT'S HOW THESE THINGS HAPPEN...

WHAT DO YOU DREAM OF INVENTING?

PATENTLY PATENTS

NOW THAT YOU'VE COME UP WITH AN INVENTION THAT YOU REALLY, REALLY BELIEVE IN, YOU MIGHT WANT TO PATENT IT. A PATENT GIVES YOU LEGAL PROTECTION TO STOP ANYBODY ELSE COPYING AND PRODUCING YOUR DESIGN.

THE WHOLE IDEA OF A PATENT IS TO MAKE SURE THAT YOU DON'T KEEP YOUR GROUNDBREAKING IDEAS A SECRET FROM THE REST OF THE WORLD - BUT SHARE THEM AND RECEIVE THE RECOGNITION YOU DESERVE AS THE INVENTOR. IT PUSHES THE WORLD OF SCIENCE AND TECHNOLOGY TO MAKE PROGRESS.

PATENTS HAVE INSPIRED AMAZING NEW LEAPS IN COMMUNICATION, EXPLORATION, AND CONSTRUCTION. WHAT NEW AREAS SHOULD INVENTORS BE LOOKING AT IN THIS CENTURY? WHAT WOULD YOU INVENT TO CHANGE THE WORLD?

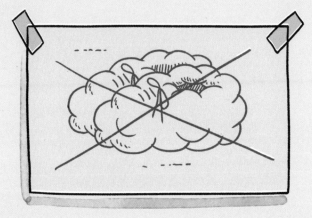

TOP TIP NO.1

CAN IT BE DONE?
TO QUALIFY FOR A PATENT, YOUR INVENTION MUST BE NEW AND BE CAPABLE OF BEING MADE - SO YOUR IDEA FOR SHOES MADE OF CLOUDS ISN'T ACCEPTABLE, SORRY.

TOP TIP NO.2

KEEP QUIET
YOU CAN ONLY APPLY FOR A PATENT IF YOUR IDEA IS A SECRET WHEN YOU APPLY. IF YOU HAVE ALREADY SHOWN LOTS OF PEOPLE, IT IS SAID TO BE 'IN THE PUBLIC DOMAIN'. SO SHHHHH!

TOP TIP NO.3

NO-GO AREAS
THERE ARE SOME THINGS THAT CAN'T BE PATENTED IN MANY COUNTRIES:
- AN ARTISTIC WORK (INCLUDING PLAYS, BOOKS AND PIECES OF MUSIC)
- A VARIETY OF PLANT OR ANIMAL
- A SCIENTIFIC DISCOVERY (AS OPPOSED TO A SCIENTIFIC INVENTION)

IMPROVE THINGS

MOST PATENTS ARE FOR AN IMPROVEMENT IN AN
EXISTING ITEM OR PROCESS, RATHER THAN FOR A
BRAND NEW INVENTION. SO TAKE INSPIRATION
FROM THE WORLD AROUND YOU. CAN YOU SEE
THINGS THAT COULD WORK BETTER? TRY TO
THINK OF WAYS THAT COULD FIX THEM!

fig 2

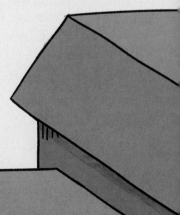

GET DRAWING

A PATENT APPLICATION REQUIRES CERTAIN DETAILS, USUALLY
INCLUDING AN OUTLINE OF ANY TECHNICAL PROBLEMS THE
INVENTION CAN SOLVE. YOU'LL HAVE TO GET YOUR CRAYONS OUT!
DRAW YOUR INVENTION, EXPLAIN WHAT MATERIALS IT IS MADE OUT
OF AND EXACTLY HOW IT WORKS.

APPLICATION FOR PATENT OF MY CRAZY INVENTION

NAME AND ADDRESS:

NAME OF CRAZY INVENTION:

CRAZY CO-INVENTORS (IF ANY):

DESCRIBE YOUR CRAZY INVENTION
IN 30 WORDS OR FEWER:

WHAT NEW WEIRD AND WACKY FEATURES
DOES THIS INVENTION INCLUDE?

ANY ADDITIONAL INFORMATION SHOULD
BE LISTED HERE:

PLEASE DRAW A DIAGRAM OR DIAGRAMS OF YOUR CRAZY INVENTION, WITH LABELS:

I REQUEST THAT A PATENT FOR MY CRAZY INVENTION BE GRANTED ON THE BASIS OF THIS APPLICATION.

SIGNED

DATE